STARTING A BUSINESS WITH ALMOST NO CASH

Disclaimer

The information is this book is provided for informational purposes only. The information is believed to be accurate as presented based on research by the author.

AUTHOR; AFEEZ CONTE

TABLE OF CONTENTS

INTRODUCTION

If you're like millions of Americans, you're dreaming of beginning your own business. Yet there are, of course, hundreds of barriers that may discourage you from ever doing this. For starters, you do not have enough energy or resources to see the research through; or you might not even have a good concept to start with — yet.

Be that as it may, where most people quit cold is their understanding that launching a business requires resources (money) which they don't have.

Nevertheless, consider: loans, grants and other financing tools, such as crowdfunding, are accessible to get you everything you need; thus, capital is not a reasonable reason not to start a business. And, beyond that, you can continue with almost no cash on other types of companies.

CHAPTER 1

WHAT'S REQUIRED TO START A BUSINESS?

The first move is to consider what's required to officially "launch" a business, and which products cost money.

Here are some of the things that is required of you to put into consideration;

1. Planning to do so. Of course, you would need to come up with a marketing strategy and financial model, so you can do that on your own, free of charge.

2. License to Business. When you're planning on forming a business, LLC or organization, you'll need to submit some documents — so it usually won't cost you more than a couple hundred bucks, based on what licenses you require. There are lots of tools in the Small Business Administration to help you find out what you need, how to access it and how much it would run.

3. A domain name. You may need to invest in the online brand early on; although I recommend that you go as professional as possible, if it is a minimum viable product, you might still take a bare-bones method to start. A catchy domain name is always all you need to identify your brand at the outset, and one can be bought for as little as $10 (if you can locate one that's not taken!). I purchase domains by making use of GoDaddy.

4. A Website. Web-builders are easy and simple to use these days. You are not going to waste anything but time building your first site. I suggest a quick start with the

commonly used website network, such as Wordpress or Wix.

5. Commercialization/marketing. Although advertisement has a reputation for being really pricey, there is really a lot of very successful strategies that can be done with only the time's money. Social networking marketing, SEO marketing and web marketing both fall into this umbrella — because, frankly, that's what you need. Entrepreneur has a great collection of books and online courses dealing with this subject.

6. Equipment. Equipment, buildings and other physical items are cash killers because they aren't required by all businesses. Any businesses may not require all of these stuffs as I will clarify shortly.

7. Products. Finally, there is something that both firms ought to market, which typically implies some initial investment. Most programs, though, may be provided with expenditure in time rather than resources.

TYPES OF BUSINESSES TO START

So, which types of enterprises should start in either of the above areas without a huge financial burden? Read on for information on the types of business idea you can start with no cash;

1. Content supplier

Websites such as Fiverr provide a fantastic platform for authors, designers, musicians, artists and video-makers to book business gigs for a range of content specifications. On the motivation and skill of an individual, the sum of money that one will produce can differ considerably. A copywriter called Alexandra Fasulo, while speaking to Entrepreneur, clarified that she began by booking tiny jobs for $5 a pop, and developed a brand and client base within two years that saw her gain six figures a year.

2. Personal creations

First up, individual inventions such as the arts and crafts are available. For examples, if you are a painter, with an expenditure of little more than art supplies and your own energy, you might sell your works of art. Platforms like Etsy, eBay and Amazon cater for designers and make it simple to transform the art into a benefit.

3. In-home services

Products because they are intangible products will not cost you much money up front. And if you operate in homes or neighborhoods that are owned by individuals, you won't need a permanent headquarters for your business. You may start a babysitting business, a dog-walking or pet-sitting business or things like landscaping or snow-plowing, for instance.

4. Repair or skill-based services

When you have a particular talent, you might use your professional labor as your business' key sales engine. If you're a handyman, for example, you might care for homeowners who don't know anything about home maintenance.

Much like in-home jobs, these kinds of gigs don't allow you to have a specific facility and don't enable you to spend in something up front, besides the materials or supplies you'll need for the work, which can range in cost.

5. Resale

The plan behind resale is simple: You buy and offer goods to others. To buy certain items, you may use dropshipping or wholesaling. You'll be delivering straight from the supplier with dropshipping (and making a smaller profit), but you still require absolutely no startup cash. You do require more resources and room up front for wholesaling but you will end up having more flexibility and more profits.

6. Consulting

Several employees dream about being businessmen even after having obtained under their belt many years about business experience. Dream about the business that you're in, and how much you've gained in that period. Up-and-coming entrepreneurs, or industry business founders, would generally be able to compensate you for your experience. Consulting is a service which only takes time to deliver which can be of great benefit as a job opportunity.

7. Micro-entrepreneurship

Of course, through micro-entrepreneurship and mutual economic incentives, you might even build your own miniature enterprise. For starters, you could drive for a business like Uber, or rent out your home via AirBnB, or other similar services that allow use of what you already have. Once you launch your business and start making money, the shortage of investment capital will turn out to be less of a concern. You may harvest and recycle the proceeds from your business, or use them to start an even bigger enterprise.

8. Social media consultant

If you developed an eye for social networking consultants? If you're a good blogger, imaginative and love to keep on top of the new developments in social networking, this could be your ideal opportunity. Many business owners either refuse to grasp the intricacies of utilizing social networking to create a reputation and grow a dedicated web audience, or they don't really know how to utilize social media at all. By providing your expertise as a social media strategist, you may either support businesses build a social networking game plan or personally gain charge of their Facebook pages and upload information on various channels.

9. Web designer

Because you learn how to create websites, you have a fairly large user base, including website developers (many of whom can establish websites but do not build them) and business owners.

If you have an eye for design but no structured web design experience, with a little informal practice and a decent portfolio, you can always enter into the field. In reality, your portfolio should be all about this industry-not your degree! That said; make sure you're just showing the best work.

10. Graphic designer

In the same way as a site designer, if you are regularly approached by businesses and individuals to create banners, merchandise bundles, social network images, brochures, posters and other products, this is a business that you would love to manage. You would have to be inspired by yourself, have an eye for information and be straightforward about setting goals.

11. SEO Expert

Search engine optimization, most generally referred to as SEO, is the process of improving web sites, ads, and other internet material so that Google and associated search engines are more likely to pick it up (and hopefully rate it highly). It is a strong future job choice for you if you are data-driven and Internet-savvy. Be sure you have a clear grip on Google Analytics, because you can possibly need it again and again.

12. Business Coach

You can enjoy this line of work if you have a knack to help people achieve success can coaching. Rather than getting employed as a contractor to help people fix challenges with their companies, by focusing on personal growth, you'll help people achieve success. It may mean understanding time control, stopping procrastination, enhancing decision-making and eventually motivating the consumers to act.

13. App Developer

Based on the findings published by the SimilarWeb's State of Mobile Web U.S. 2015, it was reported that approximately 56 percent of user traffic to leading U.S. websites originates from mobile devices. So, considering that smartphones are more common now than the internet site, if you have coding expertise it makes sense to enter this online sector.

You may either look at making your own applications as a way to earn income, or allow others to build apps. If you are eager to know more about being an software developer, you can try out some course on Udacity, or sign up for the Android App Nanodegree from Google — a fantastic new initiative that can set you apart.

14. Digital Online Store

Are you intrigued about the possibility of setting up an online shop? If it is, so you're not lonely. This is a growingly common career, rendered much simpler by the multitude of websites that will lead you through the process.

If there's something you'd like to sell, make sure you know how to set up a home-based shop, make sure you have a place to store all your products, and set up an online account with the post office to make it as quick as possible to deliver them. You may even want to look into cross-selling on sites such as eBay.

Otherwise, continue looking at sites that make it simple to sell online. You may think about Shopify, BigCommerce, Wix, and Weebly, but there are no doubt several more to choose from.

15. Virtual assistant

This job has been discussed in a number of home-based business post, but to note it is also a fantastic online business. There are a range of online platforms, including TaskRabbit, Zirtual, Upwork, PeoplePerHour and so on, that make running a VA business simple.

If you're super-organized and can execute activities easily and effectively, you may want to make use of your skills — being a virtual assistant is like becoming a personal assistant or task manager. Tools that you may provide involve project managing, blogging, running errands, doing studies, etc. Really the list is infinite.

Hopefully, you now know you don't need a lot of capital up front to start a business. You can literally launch one for just about nothing. You also need to learn what types of businesses function well under the environment.

CHAPTER 2

HOW TO BEGIN A BUSINESS WITH NO CASH

You want to be in your own business so you have little to no cash to put up as money. You are well aware that investment opportunities for start-ups are highly restricted; you might have also learned that only around 3 percent of individuals who are searching for large outside funds to begin a new business can actually receive the money they need. How are you thinking, then?

Beginning a limited-capital business needs a change of attitude. We are typically trained to continue the cycle of looking for potential business prospects by asking: "Where's a void in the market and how do I fill the gap? "A void may be an unfulfilled consumer desire, or a fresh product that has yet to be promoted.

Next, we set a target of developing a business that will fill the void. We find the money required to render our mission a possibility and to go out searching for such money. We develop a business strategy, and introduce it with the pledge of return on investment to future financiers.

If the financiers like us and like our concept, they give us the capital required to start the business. If not, otherwise we're all trapped.

Much of the time, people have trouble collecting the money they need, allowing the entire thing to crumble on its ear. There is an alternate route to a new business being developed.

Rather than beginning with the question, "There is a void in the market and how do I fill the gap? "Ask yourself," What have I got and who do I? "Take a close look at the opportunities and partnerships you have control on and evaluate whether you might bring them to use efficiently and easily in order to build a deal the customer requires or desires. You should innovate with multiple variations of tools to check how the consumer reacts to specific offerings and build a product that is very attractive to many over time.

In this method the priorities of an entrepreneur evolve over time, taking into account capital, relationships and contingencies.

These are not set at project start like they are by using the conventional method. Use the dinner party model is a helpful means of comparing the conventional and alternate forms of venture development.

Assume you are meeting a pair of mates on a Saturday evening for a relaxed sit-down meal. You may invest some time in preparation for this get-together talking about who is coming and what food they want. You might also call them up early in the week and figure out why they don't consume something, and whether they have any habits.

You'll settle on a menu after collecting this material, go to a cook book to see what supplies you need, create a shopping list and purchase the products.

You'll bring the ingredients in, cook them as instructed and ideally deliver a tasty dinner.

The option will be to get up on Saturday morning, test what you have in the refrigerator and freezer, decide what kind of food your friends want, and prepare everything with the recipes you have on hand for them.

DEVELOPING THE ALTERNATE ENTREPRENEURSHIP MENTALITY

Here are several ideas and instructions which will give you a greater chance of beginning a business with little to no money effectively.

1. Start from what you have

    At the beginning of trying to start a new business, take stock of what you have open to you. Consider your:

    - Abilities-what are you going to do?

    - Experience-what did you do in the past?

    - Knowledge-what are you acquainted with?

    - Tangible capital – what do you possess, and what exposure do you have?

    It's advised that you thought about the responses to these questions carefully. Immediately look past what comes to mind, and learn a bit more on what you have at your fingertips.

2. Take into account who you know

    Take into consideration who you meet to gain true influence and you ought to blend with who you learn. Take stock of your relationships with others, map your communication network and think how your interactions could help you to use more efficiently what you have.

    Sarasvathy points out that the alternate means of forming a business supports "stitching relationships together to build new markets." Relationships, especially equity relationships, determine the new venture's form and trajectory.

3. Save what you can afford to risk

    There's a major change in your attitude if you come from the view that "I'm saving this amount and I'm planning a return of 30 percent" and "I can afford to lose so much, so I'm going to bring it in business and see if I can make it function."

    When you've just brought in what you can manage to risk, you're leaving the business open and reducing difficulty in running it. If you're just willing to spend while you plan to get a clear gain, there's a good risk you'll never be ready to take the plunge to launch the business you've always dreamt about owning.

    An indication of that is the capitalist that wants to abandon a well-paid career until he sees an opportunity the he hopes will pay well, unlike one that chooses to spend a tiny part of his assets and two years of his life in a project that she thinks is worth the sum of time and energy – regardless of whether it will offer better than what she actually receives.

4. Experiment and adapt

    The strategic benefit of this approach is versatility and adaptability. You excel not by getting too focused on a particular target or result but by being open to environmental changes.

    Existing companies usually take longer to adjust than new businesses as they have more opportunities to maintain it the same, because they have traditions because procedures that reinforce the status quo.

The way things have already been done is not related to modern companies, and businessmen will profit from adjustments in market expectations or technological transitions or improvements in regulation by realigning their enterprises to take advantage of these trends.

As Sarasvathy puts it "there is a deliberate attempt to eliminate unexpected shocks" in the conventional approach to business planning.

The founder with the alternative mentality, "in turn, will be prepared to do about what comes their way and strive to convert all good and negative contingencies into valuable components of new prospects."

EXAMPLES OF NEW BUSINESSES YOU CAN BEGIN WITH LIMITED RESOURCES

The companies that arise when entrepreneurs have limited resources and follow the alternative attitude for new business; sometimes, they fall into one or more specific categories: operation, activities, efficiency, brokerage or schooling.

Service businesses rely on the skill and resources of the individual starting the business. Such an individual may place their talent at the fingertips of others with relatively little upfront investment. You merely need the tools of your trade to start a service business.

A consultant may need a device, some equipment from a handyman and a sewing machine from a dressmaker. You will use certain resources on hand to start marketing the business using your contacts. Event-based companies are much more nuanced but can nevertheless launch with minimal resources. Businesses that are focused on activities include projects that bring on sporting competitions, festivals and concerts. The benefit of these businesses is that through successful promotion, seats will be sold until you reach the big expenses, reducing the amount of money required to hold the business afloat.

Performance-based companies rely on entrepreneurs' abilities to succeed and bring certain people together who can boost the results.

Mark Lamberti, the visionary who transformed Makro into what it is today, claims he gained some of his most valuable management experiences in his young adult years when he performed in and directed a band.

Performance-based businesses rely on the entrepreneur's innovative abilities coupled with the opportunity to sell certain talents to a broader audience.

Musicians, actors, motivational speakers and performers also have the ability to build companies focused on the results.

Brokerage firms are among the most common forms of enterprises for those with little money. They attract buyers and sellers. Brokers through various sectors can be seen from real estate (e.g. real estate brokers), hospitality (e.g. online websites selling B&Bs), recruiting (e.g. recruiting brokers), and athletics (e.g., athletics agents putting together sportsmen and sponsors), performers and performance acts (e.g. speaking selling agents to conference coordinators) and the list goes on.

Contacting and fostering partnerships and efficient messaging on all sides of the spectrum-to customers and sellers-is the secret to being successful in brokerage companies.

Most new investment firms – including Privateproperty.co.za and Wheretostay.co.za – are already using the internet to build greater scope between buyers and sellers.

Yet the nature of business is always what it has always been, filling a void between buyers and sellers in the details. Individuals in a specific field with plenty of connections and a publicity and sales style can find a brokerage business as a low-capital route to get into operation.

Training is another field that those with little to no money pursue resources. Anyone with the knowledge and experiences many people would want to know, and an enthusiasm for helping others succeed might transition into education.

From an ex-teacher opening up a business that offers special lessons for school-going children, to a sports enthusiast starting up a coaching business, or an individual with photography experience helping others take better photos, the educational market has many low capital opportunities.

While these five market categories – operation, activities, results, brokerage, or education – can ignite any ideas inside you, they are not confined to the low capital start-up opportunities.

Through continuing technology growth, there are several new prospects developing in the field of mobile and online technologies (e.g. making smartphone apps) and in the media sector (e.g., through internet and blogging platforms, there is no longer a need to invest R5 million on building the infrastructure of a media business).

The trick is to work from what you already have – the tools you can reach, the expertise you can use and the contacts at your fingertips – to help you find out a low-cost route to a new business that is viable and profitable.

THE DRAWBACK OF THE PATH TO LOW CAPITAL

While there are several benefits to beginning the entrepreneurial journey by questioning "what do I have and who do I know?" This strategy often has its downsides and can include remedial steps to mitigate the adverse effects.

The major one focuses around the fact that the business is inextricably connected with the consumer-the consumer is the business and the business is the owner. This is impossible to expand the business in these conditions as the businessman just has too many hours a day to start providing his services.

This often is impossible to sell the business as, without the owner, it is worth so little because there is a possibility that the owner will get overworked because flame out.

To resolve these obstacles, businessmen will work on codifying what they're doing and educating others to duplicate it. We will always look at systematizing the enterprise as much as possible-developing structures and procedures to accomplish what they never should have accomplished.

The big four accounting firms both began many, many years earlier as tiny accounting companies, but they were able to expand as the senior partners successfully educated younger people who joined the business in forms of efficient accounting and auditing, and developed methodologies and procedures that could be transferred from one individual to the next to allow a larger base of people to do what they wanted.

Through putting their trading business online, Privateproperty.co.za and Wheretostay.co.za have built interest. And they are not relying on the business people to make things work. The business can be scale-up and sell without being bound to one person.

While the alternate solution to entrepreneurship has a drawback, there are also upsides too.

Focusing on what you will achieve with what you have at your fingertips is motivational and it encourages individuals to join the market in ways they would not have thought otherwise. If you're very serious about building a low-capital base business, I urge you to try it out.

CHAPTER 3

ARE YOU WILLING TO START A BUSINESS WITHOUT ANY MONEY?

Let me begin with this. It is possible to start a business which has no capital. You have an idea for a business, but you have no capital to launch it. Lack of capital is a growing reason for not beginning a venture. While some business assignment says experts to support you, if you have enough money you will have a strategy for your sector. You can start a business with no capital if you have the desire to start a business, combined with a brilliant concept and an amazing motivation to thrive. You don't require a miracle, but to effectively start a business with little capital you must take those measures.

HOW TO START A CASHLESS BUSINESS?

Young and old people say they want to start a business but don't have resources. If you have a good business plan don't let it deter you from missing money.

You may wonder "What kind of business can I start with no money? "There are a few companies that started from absolutely nothing some of them are listed below:

1. Whole Foods Market – John Mackey and Rene Lawson invested and lent funds from friends and relatives in 1978 to open their first supermarket in Austin, Texas. The two had stayed in their first shop since being evicted from their flat.

2. This all began in garages; Samsung, Disney, Facebook, Harley Davidson, Hewlett-Packard, Lotus Cars, Mattel, Yankee Candle Group.

3. Nike-Founders, Phillip Knight and Bill Bowerman began marketing their car trunk fitness trainers.

4. Dell – As a dishwasher, Michael Dell began paying a massive $2.30 an hour. Dell began selling PC from his room at the institution.

KEEP UP THE JOB

Starting a business is dangerous. It is much riskier to start a business with no capital. Don't risk the financial security of your children. The more you continue your job the fewer burdens you bring on yourself. You are not ready to walk away from a steady paycheck when you start up your business. It's real that you're going to have to work overtime because when you expand your business you will keep covering the bills. When your business is earning profits, you will start talking about turning your work off.

KEEP TO WHAT YOU KNOW

Draw on knowledge and interests. Rather than attempting to establish a business in a place beyond your comfort zone, stick to everything that you learn. Develop your business on know-how and skills. It's real you can learn different things so it's going to take time. If you wish to start a business fast, you will reflect on what you will do not years from now. Learning new techniques requires additional effort and more expenditure. You can need to take classes, receive licenses, pay contractors, etc. Starting a business in an area you are acquainted with would give you added faith.

PERFORM THE ENTIRE JOB ON YOUR OWN.

Starting a business with little resources involves having to do tasks you would usually assign to an assistant or an outside corporation.

I understand that performing the entire job on your own is stressful but you don't have the money to recruit support. Doing everything yourself you will be able to put every dollar back into your business. This would be difficult, but when you start a business with little capital that is the best way to build up a cash buffer.

PROVIDE A SERVICE

A service business is one of the best businesses that you can start with no capital. You can start a service business with virtually no cash. What you need instead of capital is the opportunity to knock on doors and create sales. Also if you choose to get a merchandise business in the end, having a service business will help you get there. To fund the dream business make use of the service sector.

Below are several wonderful commodity businesses that began selling something else: 3 M – Began as a manufacturing business. We moved on from that to market sandpaper, then to masking tape, the "Scotch Film."

Microsoft-Beginning with occasional gigs in app creation.

37signals-Beginning as site designers before developing products such as Basecamp.

Here are more than 138 service companies that you can launch today with no capital at all:

1. Start a blog-through my blog I produce income in many ways. As a skilled writer, you might develop your own business too. When you've succeeded in pushing traffic to your site the sky is the limit. You can sell ads and you can make your own items for sale. Charge to access funded content.

2. Aerial film Photography-Would you possess a drone? This may be your opportunity to turn it into an aerial photography business. They are seen widely in the real estate industry and in several other industries.

3. Affiliate marketing – Affiliate marketing is a perfect opportunity to receive a share of revenue without making a business or maintaining an inventory.

4. Alterations and tailoring – It's a perfect side business to have alteration and tailoring operation. News travels quickly as you have a competitively priced, quality service.

5. Airport transfers service – A number of people require greater versatility when it comes to airport transfers.

6. Amazon reselling – Goods will be offered through Amazon. You may import low-sell or purchase goods, and resell them. If you're loving getting amazing offers and making a profit, reselling Amazon might be a perfect business for you.

7. Antique refurbishing – The demand for antique refurbishing is a tiny area but you will create a dedicated consumer base with the right marketing.

8. Art dealer-It's not the same as buy before you break. You have to learn the importance of the artworks you interact with and the market for them.

9. Babysitting-Babysitting is not exclusively about teens. Position yourself as an Au Pair to attract a clientele with higher level.

10. Baking – You should transform your love into a nice side money making business.

11. Boat washing service – Vessels are enjoyable to have, but most people will recommend maintenance to anyone else.

12. Bookkeeping – Helping independent businesses hold their expenses in balance.

13. Brew your own beer – The hobbyists began several popular beer breweries.

14. Buy and sell domain names-You don't have to offer millions of domain names to turn them into a profitable business.

15. Business consultancy-There is a need for your business if you have expertise that can develop or run a corporation. If you are a bookkeeper, a planner, a specialist in communications, an IT guru, there are organizations out there that need your help.

16. Auto maintenance – Most people are able to spend a premium price on their own driveway and get their vehicles checked. This is a fantastic business during the weekend as well.

17. Auto flipping – It might be your opportunity to become an entrepreneur if you know how to find a lot and love working on the vehicles.

18. Carpet cleaning-Renting the equipment will launch your carpet cleaning business.

19. Catering business – This requires a lot less money to operate a catering business than to run a restaurant.

20. Cell phone repair – Instead of purchasing a new handset, several people are able to pay to patch a defective mobile.

21. Childcare-This might be a perfect business for you if you love babies.

22. Christmas light installer – While this is a seasonal business, very little capital is needed to get started.

23. Essay editor for college admissions-A perfect business if you're serious about publishing. Make sure the customers realize you're an author, so you won't write the article for them.

24. College counseling – Children of pre-college age should be directed to help them plan for what to expect at college. Through enrollment, financial aid, career counseling and other college-related subjects, you might support them.

25. Commission only sales-There are also businesses who only provide advertising incentives through reward. When you collaborate with developers, you can be willing to discuss the ownership of a portion.

26. Online lessons-On your phone, you will deliver instruction utilizing free tools such as Skype or Google Hangout.

27. Tech maintenance and repair – Many local enterprises cannot afford to employ an IT specialist full-time. If you love supporting others with computer issues, it may be for you to start an IT support services business.

28. Website quality content writing-Excellent material is what separates websites. A ton of businesses are willing to compensate a writer to build content for the website.

29. Content marketing-SEO's essence is digital marketing. Your future customers are businesses who want to boost their search engine roles.

30. Contract customer service-To many small companies, you may become the outsourced support team.

31. Copywriting and proofreading – Firms are able to outsource the proofreading to organizations beyond.

32. Custom software consultant-They appoint a custom software consultant anytime an organization needs to get specific software made.

33. Accounting – Several independent companies outsource the accounting standards. Your accounting software can help companies maintain track of their cash balance, and produce reports like P&L.

34. Dance teacher-Physical activity and a strong sense of rhythm are what you need. Awareness in several various forms in dance is a bonus.

35. Data analysis– These days, digital data is big business. As a data analyst expert, you will gain a lot with the right expertise.

36. Debt reduction service – Strong analysis capabilities will help guide those trying to popular their debt.

37. Create a mobile app – If you are willing to master the correct coding vocabulary, you will build a mobile device without needing to leave your house.

38. DJ-ing-DJ-ing can be enjoyable for a number of individuals. Throughout a group setting, perform the songs that you enjoy. When you don't mind doing most summers, evenings and holidays, this might be your business of dreams.

39. Dog walking – That is a simple work for dog owners, and can bring you a lot of activity with a moderate strength.

40. Drive for Lyft or Uber-There would be a requirement for drivers as long as vehicles are not self-driving.

41. Ebay sales – Scouring and selling bargain stores for undervalued goods on eBay may be a perfect way to make a fast profit.

42. Ebook writing – There are many niches of ebooks that will win you massive amounts of money. All you need is the ability to compose, and strong skills in science.

43. Editing business – For all kinds of purposes people use editing facilities, from college students to companies writing press releases.

44. Elderly treatment – Many elderly people require carers to check on them daily. This might be a brilliant business concept, if you're a citizen with men.

45. Executive quest-You will make huge bucks with the right expertise to support companies headhunt top executives.

46. Farmer's market – In walking distance of your home you will offer your own goods at different farmers' markets.

47. Fitness teacher – You can earn money by having people do the same because you're involved and want to stay healthy.

48. Fiverr jobs – Almost every job may be offered by Fiverr. This can be a perfect way to gain those fast earnings.

49. Furniture manufacturer-The market for personalized furniture.

50. Ghostwriting – Often people have brilliant ideas to compose proposals just don't feel comfortable in writing them themselves. Ghostwriters are bringing these theories into action and will earn a lot of money doing so.

51. Google Adwords expert – Once you know how Google Adwords functions, you'll be recruited by other businesses to collaborate with them.

52. Graphic design – As a graphic designer, you will add your creative touch into the job and create logos and other content for companies.

53. Handmade jewelry – It is another entrepreneurial venture that will earn cash for the artistic hand.

54. Handyman – A handyman performs all sorts of odd work, mainly based on fixing and building items.

55. Home appraisal – If you have the right skills and credentials, the appraisal service will be sold to homeowners who want to assess their land.

56. Home inspection service – It is common to employ a home inspector before purchasing a house.

57. Cleaning the building-this is a work that almost everyone can perform. Some people consider it very soothing to scrub.

58. House painting – everyone may decorate a house, but it is too busy for many people to decorate their own. To house painting companies there is a lot of jobs open.

59. House sitting-Home sitting is one of the best work in the country. All you have to do is stay busy in someone's home when they're gone.

60. Human billboard-Another easy work to perform. Human billboards are placed in the street carrying ads for different businesses.

61. Instagram Marketing-Sign up for a free Instagram account and know the most famous articles. That expertise can then be transformed into a marketing business.

62. Interior designer – Getting a fine taste and an eye for architecture, homeowners will employ you to prepare the interior of their house.

63. Financial advisory-You will receive bonuses and consultancy fees as an investment adviser if you have the correct qualifications.

64. Garbage removal service – When you don't like having your hands dirty, people are happy to pay to get their properties cleaned from the garbage.

65. Landing page optimizer-A perfect landing page is required for every website. A number of corporations would compensate for having the right landing page.

66. Landscape business-landscaping may be a wonderful business if you're the sort outside.

67. Massage therapy service – There is a lot of money to be made in this demanding modern world which provides soothing massages.

68. Meditation coach-Meditation is another means to relieve the real world's pain. Teaching people how to meditate will contribute to an organization free from tension.

69. Remote bike repair service – cyclists will work on this job by placing their maintenance expertise on.

70. Remote hairstylist – If you learn how to trim hair correctly, you will operate your own business in people's homes delivering haircuts.

71. Mobile make-up artist – Before major occasions including celebrations, often people like Make-up artists to meet them.

72. Mobile laundry service – Helping customers save time will be a simple way to earn money by providing a handheld laundry service.

73. Mobile mechanic-Being a mobile mechanic might be a brilliant business opportunity if you learn your way around a car motor.

74. Modeling-to excel in this industry, you don't have to look like a supermodel. Photographers and fashion brands require models for all sorts of different situations.

75. Moving service-Moving requires a great deal of physical work. People are happy to get assistance paid.

76. Music teacher-By teaching others how to play instruments, every musical talent can be transformed into a business.

77. Marketing niche-Build a website around a market. Brand it, and gain revenue from advertising. Sell the products in your own market.

78. Mobile notary public service-Offering your services as a virtual notary can be a very lucrative business idea if you have the right qualifications.

79. Cleaning of offices – Cleaning of offices requires no special training, just hard work and discipline. This business is great for nights and weekends.

80. Online dating expert-These days, online dating is a big business. This can be a great business plan to help people find love.

81. Online news reporter-As an online news editor, you can provide your services as a journalist from anywhere in the world.

82. Online Subcontractor – These days, several companies are looking for subcontract work online. That can be a very lucrative idea for a business.

83. Online training – Whatever expertise you hold can be transformed into a business by online instruction to others.

84. Patent a revolutionary invention – Listen to our Stephen Main interview whose proprietary inventions have produced billions in revenue.

85. Personal chef/caterer-There is still strong demand for culinary skills. People are recruiting chefs and caterers for special events of any kind.

86. Personal workout manager-Healthy people will operate a fantastic business and support others remain fit.

87. Podcasting-By producing your own podcast, you can transform any passion or hobby into a business.

88. Style management business-You can operate a business providing consulting services to others because you have a fantastic eye for style and management.

89. Distributor of goods – An enterprise wants the goods to meet customers. Distribution is a massive business which you join fairly quickly.

90. Proofreading – You can run a business reviewing all sorts of published documents as long as you have a clear knowledge of spelling and grammar.

91. Property management-Most tenants are too distracted or have too many assets to review any of them periodically. In doing so, property managers will operate a profitable business for them.

92. Professional mentor – If you are an involved and balanced adult with a positive attitude, you can help motivate people to accomplish fitness objectives of all sorts.

93. Personal chef – There's a massive deal of money to earn and have customized cooking services.

94. Pet care-Pet owners are able to spend big bucks to ensure sure they pose their little darlings beautifully.

95. Pet sitting-This might be a perfect business concept if you love livestock. You just have to look for dogs while the parents are gone.

96. Cleaning the pool – Many pool owners cause their pools to fester if not in operation. When the weather is correct to use the pool again, there's a massive amount of jobs for pool cleaners open.

97. Portrait photography – When you have a camera and know how to use it, there is a ton of demand for portrait photography to be created.

98. Power washing-The machine performs much of the heavy work of power washing when cleaning assets.

99. Goods/Product Photography– Businesses focus on commercial photography to make their items appear fantastic. What you need is a video for your business concept.

100. Good manager – Busy individuals will employ someone to get their day planned.

101. Programmer-design is a highly competitive profession because you have the correct skills.

102. Ebooks Publishing – You don't even need to create competencies to publish ebooks. There is a lot of income to be gained from recruiting ghostwriters to bring the concepts into practice.

103. Purchasing an actual website – purchasing an established website may be a fast way of earning money over the internet.

104. Real estate trading-Real estate is an immense business. Selling houses may be one of the best strategies for doing business out there.

105. Rent a room via Airbnb-Renting via Airbnb can be an incredibly simple way to gain some extra money if you have the space to spare.

106.   Rent your vehicle at Turo – that is another small attempt to raise any additional money. Others can continue to lease it while the vehicle isn't in operation.

107.   Residential cleaning – If they are hardworking and skilled, anybody can operate a good residential cleaning business.

108.   Review website – To earn money you should develop a review website and generate feedback like mspy review.

109.   RV cleaning service – RV owners must pay to ensure sure their vehicle is safe for everyone.

110.   SAT tutoring-Academically inclined candidates will save a lot of progress to support them obtain their SATs.

111.   Selling on Etsy – Etsy lets users offer artistic things of all sorts. It is a brilliant opportunity for the business to satisfy the creative hand.

112.   Shopping service-Customers are going to pay to spare them the hassle of getting out and purchasing things.

113.   Small business marketing specialist-You can operate a profitable business providing consulting services to small companies if you have some marketing expertise.

114.   Social media marketing expert – Individuals with strong knowledge of sites such as Facebook and Twitter can operate profitable companies advising others about how such channels should be effective.

115.　　Create a Youtube channel-For your videos you can operate a Youtube channel about any subject and eventually reach a global audience.

116.　　Stock photographer – Stock photography companies offer photographs for a broad range of uses. You will earn money by taking photos of just about every person.

117.　　Task rabbit – Staff will provide several different resources and earn money online with TaskRabbit.

118.　　Tax filing – It may be challenging to pay taxes. If you learn how to do it, there are those who can expect you to work out theirs.

119.　　Teach English online-English is becoming the industry and travel foreign language. Students from across the globe will be charging for English classes online.

120.　　Teach DIYs – When you know how to perform a job, anyone else can want to learn from you.

121.　　Tour guide – Leading visitors through your town can be an enjoyable and profitable way to share your local experience.

122.　　Translator-When you understand several languages, a lot may be created through software firms.

123.　　Disposal of garbage – Disposal of waste is a disgusting work but it can also be a very profitable business venture.

124.　　Travel planner – Organize trips to destinations that are common.

125.   Videography-You can transform images into a business with a digital camera and some directing style.

126.   Personal assistant – People use robotic assistants to handle all sorts of activities remotely.

127.   Voice over talent – Whatever the dialect, you'll usually find jobs to capture voice-over elsewhere.

128.   Website designer-Web design is a major money area provided you have the requisite expertise.

129.   Web production – Both kinds of businesses can pay for you with the correct expertise to assist in web growth.

130.   Wedding/Party/Event planner – For sociable individuals with an eye for detail this can be a nice business concept.

131.   Wedding portraits-For posterity, everybody needs to capture their wedding day.

132.   Weight loss coach-It is a socially positive and financially lucrative entrepreneurial venture to help people lose weight.

133.   Windshield replacement-Vehicles are costly, so when things go wrong, vehicle owners can spend a lot to fix them.

134.   Window cleaning-You should sell your services as a window cleaner with a pole, some soap, and a brush.

135.   WordPress website consultant – If you learn your way around the world's most famous blogging forum, there

is plenty of money to be invested as a contractor for WordPress website.

136.   Fiction writer-You should be a good writer of literature before you can make money from writing articles or books on fiction. People like Ernest Dempsey has published more than 12,000 books on the Kindle network. Bestselling author Joanna Penn of the New York Times who published more than 350,000 copies.

137.   Write holiday cards for businesses

138.   Yoga teacher– You may provide one-on-one yoga lessons or send community lessons.

BUILD A WEBSITE WHICH IS RELIABLE

If you provide some form of business service, a digital presence can help you attract more clients and bring professionalism to your business. Websites can be set up for a little expertise and expense, there are thousands of free online technical website models that will help bring the business website up in a few hours' time. It's important that you choose a reputable domain name for your website, such as your business name or your own name. Internet domain search applications such as instantdomains.com can help you save time by testing whether registration of your website name is feasible.

LET IT GO VIRAL

Starting a business with little capital involves working hard to get the message out. Don't keep a key to your business. Ask as many people as you may. Contact mates. Explain it to Members of the kin. Have it made official. Telling others allows you in a variety of areas. It'll give you extra focus, for example. Most specifically, it might help you secure any of your first clients. You may make important introductions to people in your network.

REQUEST FOR SUPPORT

You may think "I don't want to start my own business with some capital, but I don't know what to do." No one will succeed by themselves. Especially if you start a business with no capital you would need all the assistance you can receive. Small business owners branch out. Some of them went into business with little to no income.

Applying for support may benefit you in a lot of ways:

i.   Certain people in your network might be businessmen who can give you certain tips to starting a business without funding.

ii.   You might come across a co-founder. Starting a business with the right co-founder can increase the likelihood of success considerably.

iii.   A relative, family member or coworker may be able to teach you the skills you have not.

iv.   You could find office space for free.

BARTER

The bartering comes in handy when you start a business with little income. Barter your own office space expertise, goods, supplies, or facilities that you need but can't afford. In addition to this, Bartering is considered a great networking tool.

ENTER A COMMUNITY OF MASTERMINDS.

In the long run, joining or starting a mastermind group can help save you a lot of money. It offers you the opportunity to know from other businesspeople. Rather than looking for guidance to an advisor or agent, you'll connect and benefit from other entrepreneurs.

Even though many mastermind groups cost money, you are free to start your own. Look for the people in industry who are at a similar stage. You do not want to build a mastermind group of business veterans if you start. When you start reaching out to people who are also interested in starting a business and those who have been in business for less than two years; you'll get ample variety inside the party with that approach to keep things fun for everyone.

It helps if you're in the same city, but through Skype or Google Hangout you can build virtual mastermind groups, and meet.

Here are some of mastermind groups' biggest benefits:

i.   You give and get support from people with similar goals and ambitions. It can be a solitary place to be an entrepreneur. Use other people's encouragement.

ii.   Learn from those who have had some of the same or similar challenges for yours.

iii.   You can come up with different perspectives.

iv.   When you belong to a genius community the network grows increasingly increasing. Network for the community is the network.

v.   You should call for assistance because you have not encountered difficulties before.

vi.   You will be kept responsible by your fellow members.

INVENT IT TO GET IT APPROVED.

When you're an entrepreneur, you may have a corporation selling your patent. Typically you get a share of revenue of licensing agreements. The fastest way to have the idea approved is to search for distributors. Technically it's called selling the access to the patent.

You want to continue by drawing up a list of suppliers. Search at people in the market area that are already producing the items. A producer or two is not enough. Identify 25 future producers or more.

Manufacturers can be identified by gazing at product labeling, internet studies, networking and trade show visits. Libraries have outstanding fabricator position services. Thomasnet, WikiMachine, ManufacturerUSA too are possible opportunities.

Send out a brief note about your innovation to producers. Provide ample details to evoke interest, but don't overload the data. LinkedIn may be a great tool for selecting the correct person to touch.

Consult with an accomplished licensing specialist before going into talks. Ultimately, the license deal should contain specifics about cash fees, exclusivity provisions, estimates and concerns relevant to violation. In entering into an arrangement without medical help you might actually do yourself a big disservice.

PARTNER WITH BUSINESSMAN.

Solopreneurs start several businesses which quickly get overwhelmed. Most businessmen will like you to purchase yourself into a business relationship, even with little to no capital; there are still ways to do that.

You could find a business where the proprietor is about to retire. The business owner may choose to sell the business but the fact is that most companies are never selling.

The most common reasons companies are not profitable is that they are:

i.   **Unrealistically High Cost**

By the time they are classified for sale in a downward trend, and prospective customers look at the business as a dropping knife.

ii.   **Too Much Dependence on The Owner Of The Business**

Potential investors believe that, if the existing owner exits, the business will not thrive. Finding a business where the owner is either too busy or completely burnt out with the business is another alternative.

iii. **Find Capital Co-Founder**

Two or more entrepreneurs set up several productive companies. You'll still be boosting the odds of performance with two investors. Ask others in your network you're after a co-founder. They are teaming up with somebody you know. That is a little like dating.

Here are some of the ways you can lookout for potential cofounders:

i.   Colleagues, relatives, and close members

ii.   College and High School friends.

iii.   Present associates.

iv.   Regional networking activities for small companies.

v.   Enterprise sessions.

vi.   Past corporate associates, whether you have already been in business.

vii.   Operating in an environment where they operate together.

viii. Consumer teaming up.

GET PAID UP FRONT OR QUICK.

If you start a business with little to no capital, it is important that you get paid quickly. There's nothing better likely to boost the cash flow than being compensated up front. Late billing, consisting of 30, 60, or 90, will damage the business gradually.

Several forms you should get paid quickly:

i.   Apply for an advance charge of at least 50 percent.

ii.   Offer early paid bonuses.

iii.   If your clients are near, turn up in person.

iv.   Give invoices total once a week.

v.   Please allow your customers to pay by credit card or online transfer.

vi.   Get rid of customers who are persistent late payers.

vii. Automatic payment system.

ESTABLISH A LINE CREDIT.

Commonly, companies are funded through credit lines. You can wind up using a credit card to assist you with the cash flow. The problem for credit lines being that income being no alternative. Using the lines of credit just as a transitional solution, not as an option to having enough money to cover the mortgage;

LEVERAGE CROWDFUNDING.

At a moment when VCs and approved creditors oppose 98 per cent of business ventures, crowdfunding is a perfect choice for entrepreneurs. Crowdfunding needs a great deal of work and commitment, but is a fantastic choice, especially for consumer product companies. The best thing about crowdfunding is that by giving up the money, it allows you exposure to resources.

Crowdfunding will benefit you in a variety of ways:

i.   It's free!

ii.   Crowdfunding holds the investment burden down.

iii. Quick Capital Entry.

iv.   It makes you pre-sell.

v.   It's better to get crowdfunding than VC or angel investing.

vi. It gives proof of principle. When you don't get sponsored, maybe the plan isn't as brilliant as you figured it was. You should use the crowdfunding initiative as a publicity device.

vii. It will help your customers develop the business.

viii. The "crowd" delivers excellent word of mouth messaging.

ix. It will create a faithful following.

x.   It's PR Online.

The most common crowdfunding platforms are:

i.   Kickstarter

ii. Indiegogo

iii. RocketHub

iv. FundRazr

v.   GoGetFunding.

DON'T EXCLUDE YOURSELF FROM GOVERNMENT PROGRAMS

Register for support and grants through the Small Business Administration (SBA), and other federal departments. There are opportunities for mothers, veterans and minorities to fund sector.

COMPETE FOR BUSINESS STRATEGY.

Advertise the product for free. There are many places you can market your business for free, or no income, if you are able to invest it into the job. The key aspect of having free ads is that sweat equity is needed.

Here are some of the most growing free advertisement options:

i. Submit guest blog posts to the blogs in question. You'll get a connection back to your own place for free.

ii. Request Vistaprint free business cards-most notably hand them out.

iii. Establish strategic relationships with organizations that represent the same clients you seek. This will encourage you to support each other's business across borders.

iv. Set up a free Website on WordPress.

v. Register your business on Google Local.

vi. Show your business in niche-related Free Directories.

vii. Offer free review or free evaluation of the introduction.

viii. Host one event. To meet the expenses hire supporters.

ix. Build fan page on Facebook.

x. Frequent sites where hang out of your clients take place.

xi. Networking with everyone, and having unrestricted mouth ads.

xii. Ask for feedback from colleagues, relatives and individuals inside the network.

xiii. Network and support your business through social networks such as Facebook, Twitter, LinkedIn, Pinterest, etc.

xiv. Create your Day One Email list. Email is one of the most important platforms of marketing.

xv. Include your email signature on your account, Facebook profile and Twitter username.

xvi. Write an eBook or article, and use it as a gift promotion object.

xvii. Comments on blogs that have a connection back to your own pages.

xviii. Get to learn and use Search Engine Optimization (SEO) to push free traffic to your web.

xix. Create a free iPhone or Android device and add the branding within it.

xx. Register on Craigslist.

xxi. Write and publish posts specific to your specialty to content repositories.

xxii. Write and publish press release. Prlog provides online dissemination of News Releases.

xxiii. Wear ads. Print your name, URL, and telephone number on your T-shirt so people can know while you're out in the city.

For first, the above list can appear daunting but it is feasible. Taking a move at a time. Be trustworthy. Track the results, and calculate them. Rinse and repeat which ones give you the strongest performance.

EVITE MAKING RICH QUICK SCHEMES.

There are numerous examples of both online and offline "get rich fast strategies." They tell you everything you want to learn. Money fast and simple, with little to no effort. There really isn't any. You may start a business with no capital, but without hard work, critical thought and persistence you cannot start one.

Don't rely on instant success tales. They really become theories.

There are instances of true success stories and none of them is the sort of overnight:

i. Milton Hershey founded 3 failed chocolate businesses before establishing the Hershey Corporation.

ii. This took 6 years for Bill Gates to win his first job with IBM.

iii. It took 20 years for Steve Jobs to become a Billionaire overnight.

iv. It took Biz Stone 8 years for Twitter to come up with the concept.

v. It took 10 years of stand-up appearances with Steve Martin and Jim Carrey before hitting it huge.

Nothing can be more detrimental to the prospects of success than trusting in the – misleading – notion of instant prosperity. You are doing a disservice with yourself saying that. Many of the businesses need years of growth before they thrive. Without the capital, you can start a business. Expect to spend years developing your business, rather than days. Perseverance is important.

CHAPTER 4

HOW TO START A NO-MONEY BUSINESS

You have a brilliant concept and you want to turn that into starting a shop. There's one major catch here, you're cash low. Yet keeping hold of the much required funding is typically the greatest obstacle for most ambitious entrepreneurs. And how do you start your own business with no money?

Lack of capital, shouldn't stop you from chasing your business aspirations. You will do so with faith in the plan, and a simple view of how you can implement so. When you've done this, it may not be as challenging to have the funds to help your vision as it appears.

STARTING A BUSINESS

There are hundreds of millions of small companies in the US alone so it would require hard work and determination to launch a new business to succeed in that market. When you know how to operate a business and you have taken the right steps to start a business, then you should not be stopped by capital.

BEGIN A BUSINESS WITH NO MONEY CHECKLIST

i.   **Keep Your Current Work**

Practical even while you experiment around the possibility of beginning a business is incredibly necessary. Until you can start up your business, you need a steady stream of income so it is advisable to keep to your current job. You'll feel more confident when you decide to take chances while keeping your present work.

You'll need to pay more hours, of course, and work harder. But the move from becoming an employee to a business owner would be much easier, because you do not have to think about the extra expenditures.

ii. Working on Your business plan

It's only the beginning of your journey as an entrepreneur to come up with a brilliant business concept. There are lots of moves you need to take before you can launch. Some of them are to figure out your business plan and it's really important to the venture's progress.

Was your vision for the business very unique? What interest does that generate? Is it really something that the target market wants? Or do you think it's something they might want? It's necessary to get answers to these questions to decide whether the plan is effective or not.

You have a genius idea that you think is certainly going to succeed, so what about the competition? Will it be hard for a competitor to clone and repackage the proposal in a different way? If you target them for investment, a prospective lender will question you that. Knowing the environment in which you work, and the competitiveness, is quite relevant.

You will first look at the patterns and recognize the obstacles the business may face. The next move is to consider how to overcome such problems in order to stay competitive.

iii. Assess Your Capital Needs

To start your business, you need capital but how much do you really need? You run the risk of coming up with an unreasonable assessment of your business without a concrete understanding, which would scare off creditors and deny your loan application.

And before you start thinking whether you can collect funds, you can concentrate on evaluating your funding needs. How long does it take to get started? Where precisely do you use the Funds?

iv. **Explore crowdfunding platforms**

Crowdfunding sites like Kickstarter have transformed the way businesspeople collect funds to finance their new companies. Whether you choose to market a revolutionary tech application, if you want to open up an organic noodle shop, you will get people to spend.

v. **Networking with others**

It is important that you meet the right others who can support when you don't have resources to start your business. You may frequent conferences and trade shows, where new buyers can be identified. You may also participate on social networking platforms and different web groups where you can get helpful advice and tools to carry your business to life.

Many venture capitalists and investors are very involved on social networking, so if you can stun them with your concept you could find a perfect place to get your business dreams going.

vi. **Run a trial**

Would you want to see if your business plan really is unique? Take a test drive to find out. A pilot will give you the courage to move the project to the next stage and reduce the risks. You may start off on a small scale by offering a few people in your target market community some freebies to see how they react. A limited trial will provide you with some fresh ideas to grow your market and find issues you might have missed.

vii.   Gather Feedback

When you're planning on starting a whole new sector, it might really benefit if you had a second opinion from someone who understands the competition and the problems involved. When you really step into action, a business proposal that looks amazing on paper might not be so appealing. The advice of a professional will help you see stuff from a certain viewpoint and gain more information that you may lack.

viii.   Secure a Small Business Loan if Necessary

Some lending services are available to support first-time entrepreneurs develop their business. The Small Business Administration (SBA) manages the US government's proposed loan services. To order to apply for the loan, the business must follow other conditions, such as that the business must exist in the United States, your business must register as a small enterprise pursuant to SBA rules, you must work for benefit and you will have a decent credit score.

CHAPTER 5

5 DIGITAL BUSINESSES YOU CAN START WITH NO MONEY

The Web is the ultimate equalizer. Specifically in industry, it has stepped up the playing field. Anyone can start an online business earning money—anyone with a machine, that is. But here is the thing: it requires practically no technological expertise. Today you can use lots of resources to create an online business that allows the technological job much simpler than it was in the past.

You can also live wherever you want, set your own timetable, and work as little or as much as you want, depending on how fast or big your business is growing. No commercial or marketing expertise is needed either. It is a genuinely democratic medium for enterprise.

Best of all, you don't need a ton of startup money, unlike a brick-and-mortar business. You can actually get many internet businesses up and running without any money at all because there are so many free services that facilitate the possibility. For starters you can use WordPress to set up a website or blog for free. Or you can use a third-party platform such as Amazon or eBay to offer products at no expense to stock. In return you use their distribution channel to give them a share of your revenue.

And this is just the beginning of the several no-money e-commerce startup strategies open. Find five of the easiest ways to launch a business online and earn money online with minimal to no expense at all.

1. DROP SHIPPING

The fundamental premise of an electronic drop shipping business is that you don't have to hold a huge inventory (or any inventory whatsoever) of goods or do any distribution to your clients as a small business owner. Which removes the financial burden and danger of getting a warehouse full of items you might not be selling, and the difficulty of trying to ship orders around the nation or the globe; you don't even have to manufacture or store any items at all.

The last aspect you need to work on is promotion and advertisement in order to attract the clients to enable the profits. If the transaction is made other people do the rest. Your biggest disadvantage is the publicity and promotional burden of having a potential customer.

When that's completed, you should be dealing with a firm specialized in drop delivery. Here's how it works: On your page you mention items for sale or a marketplace like Amazon, eBay or Etsy.

When one of your clients makes an order, you buy the commodity at a cheaper price from a third party business (the drop shipper, typically a distributor or wholesaler). This method is as easy as forwarding the customer's request, a procedure that can potentially be completely automated. (Remember you have no chance of purchasing products here since the deal was already done). Your drop shipper would then forward the package to the consumer.

Only pretty simple, right? You may sell a large variety of goods with drop shipping, and the running costs for your business are very small.

There is no danger to your part because you can see that you don't really purchase the commodity (at cost) before the actual transaction is made!

What are the downsides to the market concept of drop-shipping?

You have to consider a trustworthy drop shipper that you can rely on for shipping to your customers. If an order is late or does not go out—or a product is of low quality—you get criticized because the business is the one who reflects the view of the supplier and the consumer.

And, since this industry is so tough, the margins — that is, the disparity between the selling prices versus how much you would offer a commodity for — are smaller, and it's going to be a high-volume style business to make a real profit. But still, it is a low to no-cost startup choice that is worthwhile.

Another approach to differentiate the goods from the market for a drop shipping business is through private marking. This basically indicates you're placing your own label/brand on the items the supplier makes. That way, you're not offering the same range of goods so you're only relying on the price; you can choose your own name instead and meet fewer pressures. Think of when you glance at the pharmacy's medicine; the big labels sell at better costs because people believe they're distinct than the cheaper ones, even when the products are almost the same. When searching for a successful drop shipping deal, consider these essential factors.

Anyone planning a drop shipping business will start seriously using Amazon.com to expand their business and know more about being a successful Amazon retailer, since Amazon is a proven platform that customers now trust and have a strong consumer base. You should also finally start getting your own online shop too.

Pros

i. Needs relatively few money for startup

ii. No need to hold inventory

iii. You can exploit proven marketplaces and large client bases

Cons

i. You will be criticized for the errors made by the drop shipper

ii. It is a competitive market

iii. You have to sell a lot to earn significant profit

2. AFFILIATE MARKETING

Affiliate marketing is very similar to drop shipping, albeit with several main variations. Again, in this e-commerce platform, you don't have an inventory of your own goods, so you don't have to think about delivering items to clients.

Basically, you're picking a lucrative niche for your online market, and instead you'll find an associate partner who has goods in that niche. Many of the more common partner sites include Clickbank.com, Amazon.com, and Conversant's CJ Affiliate (formerly Commission Junction). They sell within them just about any interactive content tool (such as ebooks, audio files, video files) or any tangible tool you may think of. Can major names and retailers like Wal-Mart, Home Depot, etc. run their partner services from certain partner pages of third parties.

You sell the items for sale through affiliate ads, for example on your forum or e-commerce website. Business has a unique connection, which monitors your associate partner back to your account. For checkout, a possibility who clicks on the connection would be brought to your partner's shopping cart. When they order, they report the transaction and you get a fee. Commission rates differ depending on the associate party, but are usually 5% to 25%, or 50% or more, for interactive content items. As you can see, there is no danger on your side and basically no need for expenditure either. Much as with drop delivery, publicity and advertisement would be the only costs to push traffic and produce selling.

The main distinction between this and drop shipping is that there are far more hands off on the business model. What you have to do is have a connection for the consumer to click on and the retailer manages everything; payment, order delivery, customer support, etc. Everything you have to do is control the messaging to encourage the customers to purchase (through social networking, email marketing, tweeting, or whichever tool you choose). However it is out of your reach after they click on the affiliate button. You don't have to mail goods or answer any issues about customer support. Most definitely, you don't have to maintain an inventory. What you need to do is concentrate on paying and free forms to advertise your business online. Affiliate marketing is really one of the most 'hand-off' online business styles you may launch.

Pros

i. Low risk: No upfront expenditure needed

ii.   Hands-off business model

Cons

i.   You are liable for moving site traffic to the affiliate link (no traffic equals no revenue)

ii.   Will have to expend money on ads and promotions

3. BLOGGING

You're ready to start making money with a blog if you have the skills or a passion or curiosity for a subject. You can launch your blog fully free with a service like Blogger (www.blogger.com) you may even build your own website and guarantee your own hosting for a cheap price, which is usually the path I prefer, because many free blogging platforms have limits on what you may post or do, like earning money or advertisement.

You might assume that blogging is just about posting. So if this is what you intend to do, and then it will be. Yet Blog posts posted are only the beginning. You can add images, videos, and links to other blogs, you can also repost news and other posts ... everything is fair, actually, so long as it corresponds to your niche.

They're essential to publishing original content that's relevant to your target market and updating it consistently. This is the perfect way to rate in the search engines and encourage the followers to take action as well.

What kind of content will you be offering? All that interacts with your   prospects.   How-to-themes,   top-10   lists,   regional developments insight, tips and tricks articles — basically, you need to have valuable material. Your site is not short in concepts. In an online business site you'll make money in a lot of ways.

i. Google AdSense.

Have you ever viewed a website and noticed an ad thereon? It's possible it was an ad going via Google's advertisement network. Such pay-per-click ads run on your blog. Any time anyone clicks on an ad (which is intended to be about a niche-related topic), you're getting a few cents or more. Each time, tiny numbers, nevertheless add up. It is incredibly hands-off. Only get a link from Google, put it on your website-and the advertisements will show automatically on your page. Google can only view commercials that are important to your blog and it's a nice experience for your users and maximizes the amount of views you receive, which means more sales.

ii. Blog ad Networks.

You may also partner with non-Google ad networks, including Blogads, to display banner ads on your blog. Same as Google Adsense advertising, you place the application on the website once and then you get charged when the guests click on the advertising. You can also display video advertisements on your blog, in addition to banner advertising.

You may earn more money with blog ad networks in many situations, but they appear to only operate for blogs that receive tens of thousands of users a month or more; as compared to Google Advertising where you can launch automatically irrespective of how much traffic you attract.

iii. Affiliate Marketing

You do know it. You have ties to the goods that you advertise as an associate and you get a discount each time anyone buys the product. You will combine ads with material with a forum and make things much more possible that you would be receiving the deal. For e.g., you might do a summary of the product—which is helpful content—and instead add a connection to purchase the product under a link to an affiliate; there are a few good writing ideas to insure that readers will locate your blog — and will continue to come here often. This is crucial to developing your blog and making it a successful business.

i. You ought to be engaged in the delivery of usable content.

ii. If your blog is dull, or you can find the details online, nobody would read it. Feel free to bring your own style on the site.

iii. You have to publish material regularly.

iv. People are thirsting for the fresh, so make sure you regularly put up posts, videos or whatever. This may be one post regular, or three days a week. Whoever it might be, stick to the same timetable. A past of scattershot publishing implies losing followers.

v. At least seek to plan a week with one new message, video or other types of material.

Don't fake it.

Yeah, you can make money out of your blog. Yet you cannot always render advertisement appeals. Focus on valuable content so your followers get to know you, enjoy it, and trust you. Then of course they can click on your ads or purchase the items that you suggest. People are finding credibility in this age of the Internet and social media.

Achieve all that, and you'll be catching the interest from search engines like Google who are constantly trying to place pages with valuable, important material on top of the search results. This is more about the web marketing.

In less than an hour you might launch a blog. Even as you build readership, it takes time to raise profits, so just a limited number of those people end up purchasing your goods.

Pros

    i.   Really small start-up costs

    ii.   You will be operating with your own terms

Cons

    i.   Producing and uploading content may take a long time

    ii.   To start earning money may take long time as well.

4. ONLINE VIDEO

Did you see a new YouTube video? You have of course! This is one of the most popular web pages in the world, with over 1 billion viewers viewing hundreds of millions of hours of content every day. And by some chance it's not just cats doing humorous stuff.

You can exploit the power of YouTube on internet to earn money. No, you're not, so to say, attempting to make a viral picture, but though it spreads all over the place and is watched by millions, that's a positive thing.

Instead, you'll consistently adopt a validated technique to increase views of several videos images. You can build interesting content—something that viewers want to see talking in. And this fits in several specific niches, very special. It might be a quick how-to or a talk-head quick about a subject of interest to people in your niche — the sky's the limit.

You're getting money from the ad sales. Your first move is to start posting videos and build a YouTube account. You then allow monetization in your YouTube settings. This essentially offers Google the go-ahead to display the videos with quick AdSense advertising, which you've seen if you've seen a YouTube video. You get paid when audiences click on such advertisements.

Another opportunity to earn money is by paying sponsorships for a YouTube site. Create up a big enough follow-up and corporations are more than willing to pay for endorsing or including their goods and services in your posts.

Any ideas for making professional-looking videos (not needing costly pro equipment): You can use your mobile or a basic device. But make sure the lighting is perfect, so that you can see everything in your video plainly and easily. Make sure that the recording is clear. You don't like a buzz of air conditioning, construction noise or other disturbances. Using basic editing tools such as iMovie to place titles at the start of the frame, and delete any flubs. Mind, above all, that your videos can be easy, and need not be sleek. Only have valuable material, and be fun and entertaining. Makes Amusing, too.

And to extend your videos' scope, make sure to share them on your Facebook business page, Instagram, blog and other platforms. Let people realize that you are now in the video market. You can even use your YouTube channel to bring traffic back to your website in addition to ad income from YouTube videos, where people can read your product reviews, press the advertisements on your page, or even go to your email newsletter list — which you can create several purchases from your email list.

Pros

    i.   You will use same mobile device or computer.

    ii.   It operates in many specific niches.

Cons

    i.   It can be time-consuming to make and upload videos.

    ii.   Making of money can take a longer period of time

5. INFORMATION PRODUCTS

This does not have to be about selling physical goods when you have an internet business. Digital information are probably one of the simplest and cheapest ways to earn money.

There is no lack of ways to produce knowledge items, but the most common types include: audio: a filmed teleconference, lecture, tutorial, or any other spoken word product Video: a documented webinar, a how-to, a lecture Text: an ebook, any sort of training booklet, a travel guide For any of these categories, you can really get inventive and render any kind of format and style.

It's passive profits, no matter if you do it – money you receive when you're asleep and you placed these items on your website for sale so a buyer can purchase and access them instantly at any time of day or night. All you have to do is regularly review the sales and see what subjects or forms of items are better sellers and you can create one of those.

Pros

i.   May pull in passive profits after you place the goods on the market

ii. Would be a fast way to earn money

Cons

i.   Producing a business needs some hard effort and time

ii. You will need to potentially spend some capital

Getting it all together

The trick for any online business is to make sure you're in a lucrative area. And make sure to keep an eye on sales, check out bestseller lists on platforms like Amazon and worry about what people are thinking about on social media. One point to bear in mind is that you don't have to confine yourself to only one of these possibilities for e-commerce. Start with one, and get it to function. Then introduce additional sources of sales, because you may. That's going to boost your profits and make sure you have plenty to fall back on in case one business begins heading south.

CHAPTER 6

HOW TO START A BUSINESS WHEN YOU BASICALLY HAVE NO RESOURCES

You don't really need a ton of funding to start a business. You will really get going even with little or no money. (Yes!) Running a business without capital may sound like a far-fetched concept at first, but it is not impossible. It's real that you are going to need more than just extra cash flow to start and grow every business. You'll definitely need associates, promoters and a sound strategy for how to use your new business funds to expand. Nevertheless, you start tiny because you're only starting out. Even better: As tiny as you want you can continue.

You can also continue by selling them to friends and family if your intention is to open a shop where you sell your hand-crafted products. You should be able to develop credibility and get initial reviews. You will then offer them digitally on a third-party web platform. Before that, you should switch on to hosting and storing your own account. You get the clear image.

In the event that you're worried about how you can start a business with no funds, below are few helpful ideas on where you can start.

i.   **Tell yourself everything you should do to get away.**

A list of challenges getting in the path of beginning the business is quick to come up with. Sometimes it is more complicated to come up with a number of possibilities that are right before you. If you're frightened by the prospect of beginning a business without money, pause and focus about what you can do without right now.

ii.   **What's so important to your business?**

Require the custom-designed sleek website when you've polished only three products for your latest store? Could you build a Facebook account, instead, to advertise your business locally? Or, does it make more sense to add the goods on a platform like Etsy for sale? Does it make more sense to get your own marketing materials built on Canva? Could you barter and swap your skills/products/resources instead of charging for anyone else?

To claim that the site includes a ton of free tools is an underestimate. Make a list of what you need for your business, and then find free web-based alternatives. It can take time, and maybe even demand that you pick up any additional technical skills, so when you need them most, you can save money.

iii.   **Built up six months of cost savings**

Obviously, dipping into your investment plan is not the perfect scenario. It's, however, a pretty popular activity among entrepreneurs. Be honest with yourself while developing a marketing strategy on how much you are investing, and how much money you are going to pull in. Then, be honest on how long it takes to make a return. It normally takes about six months before you begin to see some cash pouring in. Consider it a priority to save living costs for at least six months so you can contribute to your new business.

iv.   **Ask your friends and relatives for extra funds**

Note you don't press for charities. You don't expect your buddies and relatives to back up your wacky business proposal. No, you have a corporate vision and your business strategy is a good one. You're circling the t's and dotting the I; that's why when you're doing the presentation, you're aiming for people closest to you. Making use of family and friends as multi layered tools.

v.   **Train them for the sales speech.**

Request reviews. And, when you're about to launch your business, make inquiries if they can help kick-start the business with a small loan. Please make sure to note down all and when you will make paying them back. You may also use a crowdfunding website to inspire the people around you to invest in their network.

vi.   **When you need more funds, apply for a small business loan**

If you are searching for more money and have been working on a shoestring budget, suggest applying for a small business loan. Banks and private providers provide different kinds of small business loans to clients searching for increased cash flow or savings funds. In a conventional branch, you will normally get more attractive terms. Nevertheless, online borrowers are usually more indulgent in their requests. Beware of such heavy interest levels.

vii. If you aren't searching for a lump sum loan number, make credit line business. In short, to your business they are like credit cards. They're nice as-needed choices for purchasing products. Look at small business grants and local funding incentives Real, small business grants aren't necessarily the simplest to locate or receive. But, once you get your business up and running (no matter how small), you can start looking for free cash in earnest. Note also that grants typically include unique criteria for proposals. So long so you reach those, you are racing for a pot of cash which is all yours to collect. Begin your quest in government directories, and please be sure to ask for guidance from your local organizations on small business management.

viii. **Find more about — and woo — potential angel investors**

You've already heard about, and for good cause, angel investors. Once it's time to expand the business past you, yourself and the handful of loved ones who've invested in, they come into action. Angel investors are usually among the first individuals to participate in a business outside the corporation. Unlike large companies like other investment firms, angel investors are depositing their own specific assets. These can also make them the strongest kind of advisors, since many are themselves former/current businessmen.

SUMMARY

In the event that you find yourself among the millions of people all over the world with the dream of where to begin your own business; yet there are, of course, hundreds of barriers that may discourage you from ever doing this. As a starter, you could be thinking that you need millions of cash to kick start your own business, but quite no; that is not the case, this book as explained everything you need to know about starting a business with no cash.